I0146630

Elhanan Winchester Reynolds

The Relations of Slavery to the War

And the Position of the Clergy at the Present Time

Elhanan Winchester Reynolds

The Relations of Slavery to the War
And the Position of the Clergy at the Present Time

ISBN/EAN: 9783337402143

Printed in Europe, USA, Canada, Australia, Japan

Cover: Foto ©ninafisch / pixelio.de

More available books at **www.hansebooks.com**

THE

RELATIONS OF SLAVERY TO THE WAR:

AND

The Position of the Clergy

AT THE PRESENT TIME.

———— ◆ ————

THREE DISCOURSES,

PREACHED AT WATERTOWN, N. Y.,

By Rev. E. W. REYNOLDS.

———— ◆ ————

WATERTOWN, N. Y.:

SOLD AT THE BOOKSTORES AND AT RAND'S.

1861.

For Civil War, that it is an evil I dispute not. But that it is the greatest of evils, that I stoutly deny. It doth indeed appear to the misjudging to be a worse calamity than bad government, because its miseries are collected within a short space and time, and may easily, at one view, be taken in and perceived. . . . . . When the devil of Tyranny hath gone into the body politic, he departs not but with struggles, and foaming, and great convulsions. Shall he, therefore, vex it forever, lest, in going out, he for a moment tear and rend it?—MILTON.

——It is impossible for a nation, even while struggling for itself, not to acquire something for all mankind.—MOTLEY.

Whatever is just, is always true law; nor can true law either be originated or abrogated by any written enactments.—CICERO.

Tyranny is against the law of nature.—ARISTOTLE.

Slavery is introduced through human wickedness; but GOD advocates Liberty by the nature he has given to man.—BLACKSTONE.

WHAT IT MEANS.

A brief word, by way of explanation, will account for the appearance of this Pamphlet.

The first Discourse having been delivered, agreeably to previous notice, it appeared that a few persons were displeased—the disaffected being of two classes: 1st. Those who disliked the topic too much to allow them to hear the sermon, and who,—*assuming* that the TREATMENT would be objectionable,—were willing to derive their impressions from report, merely. 2d. Those who attended that service *expecting* to dislike the address, and who heard without apprehending—as appears from their subsequent statements.

My best defence, against misapprehension and misconstruction, appears to be to lay the Discourse before those who may feel any interest in the subject, in the form in which it was actually delivered.

The other Discourses have grown out of the first; and are included in the publication because they were designed to illustrate and fortify the more radical sentiments originally expressed.

The Sermons will be found not so much *echoes* of public opinion, as *intimations* of a sentiment destined to assert itself triumphantly, if I mistake not, in a few months, in American politics. If the pamphlet should happen to be read by those not yet prepared to accept its teachings, let me request them to suspend their final decision until the events now pending shall have spent their force on the public mind.

I have heard it objected, that any agitation of the Slavery question, in the present crisis, is injudicious, because tending to revive party divisions and divert attention from the business immediately before us. In relation to the objection, I regard the people of the Free States as already decisively committed to the War; the Government will be sustained, and the Union will be preserved; and the thing we shall soon be obliged to decide, is, What to do with the Arch Criminal that has made all the mischief? I agree with gentlemen who say that when the house has been set on fire, the first necessity is, to smother the conflagration; but I beg to remind them, that the next dictate of reason and self-preservation, is, to set the police on the INCENDIARY, in order that we may never incur the like calamity in future.

E. W. REYNOLDS.

May 21, 1861.

I.

SLAVERY,

RETROSPECTIVE, ACTUAL, AND PROSPECTIVE.

Remember the days of old.—DEUT. xxxii, 7.

There is always profit in recurring to the Past, if the retrospect be intelligent, and the view comprehensive. In that case, the wise man will find, in the surviving memorials of human history and experience, much pertinent instruction,—much to admonish, to encourage, and to guide. For humanity, in its various phases, and in its widest extremes, is impressed upon "the days of old." In its records, the rival principles that have always divided the world, and that still enlist the interest and power of mankind, have left the traces of their essence, their influence, and their results.

What can be more impressive or instructive, than to reanimate past ages, and to see the passions which we have espoused, or the passions against which we are marshalled in conflict—displayed in their true nature, and ripening their legitimate fruit? For History repeats itself, from age to age, from land to land,—like the splendid sunsets that embellish the West, and like the tornadoes that darken the tropic seas. A few great principles, beneficent and divine—and a few great passions, pernicious and human—have furnished the materials of all the conflicts in which the nations have participated, and which it is the business of universal history to describe. Dip into what annals we will,—grope back to an antiquity however remote,—revive the concerns of a people however obscure or strange,—and we come, at once, upon these familiar elements of our nature, that are playing in our latest politics, and coloring the character of every living man,—these indestructible elements, which Divine Providence is weaving into a succession of dramas, for the vindication of Justice and Truth, for the discipline and perfection of the world.

If it be instructive to recur to "the days of old," in times of social tranquility, how much more so must be the retrospect, when Society is agitated and confused,—when the Government is assailed by Anarchy—when delirious passions eclipse the serenity of reason—when the present scene is too much darkened by the smoke of the combat to admit of distinct impressions; and when we are thrown back upon the Past for solid footing, and for a serene, unbiased wisdom. There are facts and experiments, impressed upon the olden days, well qualified to enlighten us in our duty, and to admonish us of our dangers, in the critical times upon which we are cast. I shall endeavor, on this occasion, to bring to light such facts, or such experiences, out of the Past, as seem qualified to subserve the purposes of an enlightened patriotism, in the present crisis of affairs.

In re-reading Macaulay's History, recently, I was struck by the fact, that the great social Evil, which, in this country, has been the occasion of so much discord and the spring of such imminent danger—was abolished, in the English nation, not only without violence, but without notoriety. In the Thirteenth Century, Slavery was universal in England; but, by the Fifteenth or Sixteenth Centuries, it had entirely disappeared from the realm. Yet, this great social revolution seems to have gone silently forward, involving no great controversies, and attracting no special attention from cotemporary observers. It became the object of no legislative enactments, and it provoked no physical force; but it *faded* out of the civilization of England under the intensifying power of moral causes, and no man can tell, precisely, at what period it ceased to stain the web of Society.

If we inquire for the causes that produced that great change, in so peaceful a manner, and by such imperceptible degrees, we shall find that the main cause was the feeling of the Church, touching the institution of Slavery. The Christian Church, from the beginning, in all countries, had been hostile to the practice of slave-holding. It had uniformly made its power felt, in mitigating or restricting the Evil, as fast as it became strong enough to make its authority respected. The idea of possessing property in Man was repugnant, from the first, to the fundamental ideas of the Gospel; and there is hardly an illustrious name on the roll of the Church, that is not associated with some protest against Slavery, or with some effort for its abolition. Since this was the common sentiment that swayed the Christian teachers, it followed, naturally enough, that soon as the Church obtained ascendency over a tribe, or nation, it should bring its power to bear, persistently and inflexibly, upon the unjust distinction of Master and Slave.

This was really the case; and another thing to be noted, is, that the Church, in the Middle Ages,—not only in England, but in all the countries of Europe,—had all but absolute *power* to execute her purposes. Those who professed Christianity, believed implicitly that the Church held the keys of Heaven and Earth, and could admit the dying to endless bliss, or banish them to endless pain. In that rude age, when the Norman lords were above the restraints of Civil Law, and their vassals below its protection—the only hope of the weak, was in the power of the Church, which could bless or damn the soul of the haughtiest baron. Generously and nobly, in most instances, did the priests use that terrible engine of Superstition. When the great Norman chiefs lay in the agonies of death, the blessing of the Church was of more value than all the crowns of the world; and when that blessing was made dependent on the instant liberation of those boundmen for whom Christ died, the parting sinner was not likely to hesitate where duty and interest so palpably met. So faithfully did the Christian teachers employ their tremendous ecclesiastical influ-

ence, for the benefit of Society, that Slavery became utterly
exterminated in England, and the servile class elevated into
manhood, before the advent of the Reformation. And so
unquestionable was the agency of the Ancient Church in
achieving the salutary revolution, that Sir Thomas Smith—one
of the ablest Protestants in the court of Elizabeth—bears the
strongest testimony to the fact.

Although NEGRO SLAVERY, a century or so later, prevailed to
some extent in England, it never received the general sanction
of the Courts; and, in the celebrated decision of Lord Mansfield, made in 1772, it was shown that no slave could be
retained, against his will, by the law of the realm. Slavery
was a condition so "odious," in the language of Lord Mansfield's decision, that nothing could be suffered to support it
but positive law; and that support it never had from the law
of England, either in Britain or in the Colonies.

In America, when the Church was brought face to face with
Slavery, at the organization of our Government, the combat
was to be waged under different circumstances. Society had
undergone great changes, since the Middle Ages; and some
of the changes were adverse, and others were favorable, to a
successful contest with Slavery. The Reformation had broken
that iron machinery of the Church, which had been so service-
able in former times; and it was our weaker Protestantism
that had to grapple with the American slave-holder. Religion
had ceased to be that stern and palpable "terror to evil-doers,"
which it had been when the Priest was supposed to hold the
keys of Heaven; and it could not, therefore, exert as vigorous
a restraint. On the other hand, the progress of Society had
widened and confirmed all those sentiments of humanity, which
are hostile to Slavery. The Institution had become, from generation to generation, more and more odious. The tendency of
all History, from the opening of the Reformation onward, was
to render every form of tyranny unpopular,—to unsettle the
old wrongs,—to inspire sympathy for those struggling for their
rights; and to create lively anticipations of the rapid spread
of Liberty over the world.

Such were the circumstances under which the American Church, eighty years ago, was summoned to encounter that great anomaly of our republic—American Slavery. I say that the CHURCH was summoned to encounter this Evil,—not forgetting, however, that the State Governments, and the Federal Convention, were also agitating the subject; and that Slavery provoked, from the first, the resolute opposition of most of our revolutionary statesmen. But, from the nature of the subject, Slavery had always been regarded as pre-eminently a *moral* subject,—as something over which RELIGION had peculiar jurisdiction; and as a wrong on the nature of man, so patent and notorious, that the Christian teachers must, as a matter of course, strive unremittingly to have it done away.

Nor did the conflict, at first, threaten to be very severe. The predominant sentiment of the nation was an anti-Slavery sentiment, and it found a calm and strong utterance from Virginia to Massachusetts. Only in the Carolinas and in Georgia, were there indications of a settled devotion to Slavery, or a determination evinced to perpetuate it, at all hazards. The great body of influential men, in other states, esteemed Slavery as a blot upon the nation; and their sympathies and convictions were heartily opposed to its perpetuity. Such being the state of public opinion, it seemed every way probable that such influences would emanate from our Government, and especially from our Churches, as to involve, at no distant day, the peaceful removal of the one great Evil that impeded our social progress. Unexpected developments disappointed this reasonable expectation. The manufacture of Cotton rendered slave-labor profitable in the Gulf-States, and opened a lucrative commerce in slaves, for the states of the Interior. At the same time, the acquisition of new Slave Territory, gave a broader base to the Institution, on which to resist the humane, freedom-loving public opinion of Chistendom.

Then came the trial of the vigor of the American Church. When the tide of Improvement began to set backward, then was the time for the Church to have thrown all its power against the ebbing waters. When a great Temptation came

2

to stimulate the lust of the nation,—when temporal Gain was set before the Eternal Right, so that the contact of wealth and luxury might dazzle the eye and seduce the conscience,—then was the time for the Church to revive the image of Liberty, of God, and of responsibility. When Slavery began to reveal its despotic purpose,—when, not content with the subjugation of the black man, it assumed to domineer over the white,—when it proceeded to crack its plantation whip over Congress, to bully timid statesmen, and to gnash its teeth against the bold champions of Freedom,—then was the time for every pulpit to blaze with the lightnings of Divine Truth, and for every Christian man to invoke the Almighty Name, till the nation should be awake to its peril, and the moral apostacy of the land rebuked.

The American Church was not equal to the emergency. It bent before the roaring beast it ought to have taken by the horns; and it apologized for the system which even a Deist had pronounced "the sum of all villanies." That sacred INSTITUTION which Jesus Christ had founded among men, as a refuge for the weak,—as the hope of the merciful,—as the means of breaking every yoke, and setting every captive free,—even *that* humbled itself before the arrogance of Slavery, and held its peace; while Liberty fell in the streets, and Honor veiled her face. It was the saddest, most shameful, most perilous day of our history, when the Christianity of this land was bribed and badgered into submission to Slavery. No—there was a sadder, more shameful, more perilous day even than that: the day that the most venerable bodies of the Church conspired to pronounce Slavery divine, and to stigmatize as Infidels, the faithful men who suffered for freedom!

I suppose it is now clear, to the minds of American freemen, that the Church committed a great error, if not a great crime, in having made any terms with Slavery. If the pulpit and the religious press had refused to compromise with slave-holding,—if the Churches had excluded slave-holders from the communion,—if every minister, ordained to the service of Christ, had labored to array this wrong before men under the odium of

Divine condemnation,—it could not have been perpetuated to this day. The voice of Religion would have so ratified the moral convictions of our people, and lent such authority and vigor to the best feelings of our nature, that Slavery would have been extinguished, peaceably and imperceptibly, by a process similar to that which eradicated it from England. With vigorous moral causes working for its removal, the subject would have entered less into our politics,—it would have had little or no opportunity to vitiate the Government,— the rancorous hostility between the North and South would have been averted, and Treason would never have dragged our flag to the dust.

The moment the Church consented to ignore, or tolerate, the enormous sin, Slavery began to be dominant in our politics, and the Government began to be prostituted to its purposes. In private circles, it became fashionable to apologize for Slavery, and to deny or extenuate the abuses which the system involves. In public life, the path of ambition became the path of subserviency and compromise. This despotism came to possess the offices and the honors of the Republic, and it dispensed them to those who could abase themselves most, as the tools of its wicked policy.

While the masses of our people were thus yielding to the disastrous retrogression of public opinion, a small band of earnest men, whom the popular sophistry had not infected, rallied to the standard of Liberty. Through calumny, persecution and violence, they kept their ground, and made their voices heard through the land. They have never been a very lovable set of men; for in Politics they have been as stern as the sternest Puritan—and in Religion, lax as the most speculative Rationalist. They have dealt in the severest language; they have advocated the extremest measures; they have courted the hatred of Church and State. But, they have been, as a party, a sort of providential break-water against an overflowing political apostacy; and, when the history of the last thirty years shall be honestly written, the Garrisonian party will occupy, perhaps, as honorable a place in our annals, as the Puritans already occupy in the annals of the Stuarts.

Meantime, the development of the slave-holding despotism has borne such fruit as no man foresaw who consented to tolerate its growth. The effects of the system have been so palpably *retributive*, as to evince a Divine agency working out its destruction, if not the destruction of those leagued with it. We are too much in the habit of estimating the evils of Slavery, with reference to the Negro race. Its direct and obvious effects upon the slaves themselves, are, doubtless, revolting enough, in many instances; but the most terrific effects of the system appear, not in its results to the negro, but in its results to the white man. Slavery may not be an obvious injury to every individual slave; but I maintain that it *is* an obvious injury to every individual master,—to every free family,—to every State, and to the very *life* of the Republic. Forty years ago, actuated by commercial selfishness, and by our antipathies to the African race, we supposed that the perpetuity of Slavery would damage nobody but the helpless negro. But, behold how God has punished our cruelty, and confounded our expectations! The African race, in America, has passed through a baptism of fire; but it has multiplied, as the Israelites did under the oppressions of Egypt. It has become a more civilized and mighty race; drawing from its task-masters more mental vigor, and greater relish for freedom, from year to year, till it has become a terror in the land, no longer to be trusted, hardly to be restrained.

While God has thus been strengthening the servile race, He has been weakening their oppressors. While the negro has been rising toward Civilization, the white man of the South has been sinking into Barbarism. Ignorance and Superstition, Cruelty and Vice, Violence and Anarchy, reign paramount in the slave-holding States. There never was seen such a sudden and wholesale relapse of great communities into hopeless barbarism. The records of the social life of those States has been, for some years, like pages gathered from the annals of the Tenth Century. Such violent despotism over private judgment,—such sanguinary sway of lynch law,—such subjugation of cities to brutal mobs, and of States to revolutionary anarchy,—such swaggering pretensions to honor and chivalry, united with crimes that only the hangman can properly punish,—such spectacles which make up the every day life of the South, almost persuade a man that he is reading a chronicle of the Middle Ages, and not an American newspaper, reporting contemporaneous events.

As little did we foresee the effect of Slavery on the safety and integrity of the American Government. When it clamored for protection, we never thought it would aspire to rule. When it aspired to rule, we never thought it would conspire to ruin the Republic if it were voted out of power. But, such is the nature of the system, that it makes everything it touches *subservient ;* and, soon as it comes to be resisted, breaks every treaty, defies every consequence, and malignantly stabs the nation that has warmed it into power. Itself based upon injustice, rapine and cruelty, it is not conciliated by fair play, or restrained by considerations of social well-being, or affected by the prospect of boundless carnage. It is a creature of lust, aggression and violence; and its legitimate influence is always fatal, just in proportion to its power and opportunity.

With the nature and tendencies of Slavery so clearly disclosed, as they now are, in the state of Southern society and in this most wicked Rebellion, if there is an American freeman who can apologize for it any longer, it must be a case of infatuation utterly without parallel. And if this bloody quarrel, which Slavery has ruthlessly provoked, is ever settled without rooting the deadly curse out of the land, we shall bequeath a new quarrel to our children, and untold calamities to mankind. We were willing to tolerate Slavery, from a sense of constitutional obligation ; and we would even violate conscience to keep the faith our fathers were believed to have bound us by. But, since Slavery was not content with being tolerated, but insisted on being our dictator; since she will be our autocrat or our destroyer; and since she has taken down the sword and summoned us to mortal combat—away with all forbearance, and all compromise, and let the wicked harlot die. She has released us from the old compact, whatever *that* may have involved; and God be thanked for the madness of despotism that has broken the dangerous bond. She has exasperated every freeman, by forty years of insolence,—by forty years of broken faith and culminating crimes; and now by the just God in Heaven, and by the holy instincts of Freedom, she shall perish by the sword she has compelled us to draw!

We have endured everything from Slavery that human nature can endure, beause our temper is forbearing, our manners pacific, and our pursuits compatible only with peace. We have consented to be a reproach to civilized nations, because of our complicity in this great wrong. We have consented to bear more than our just proportion of the burdens of Government, and have received less than our just share of its emoluments. We have submitted to have our citizens mobbed, imprisoned, and hung, for no crime but that of being born in a Free State, and loving their natural birthright. We have endured insults and aggressions, fraud and violence, in the halls of Congress, and in our own free cities. We have given up the weak to the fangs of the slave-hunter, and seen the mark of the beast set upon the forehead of our most illustrious men. All this has not been enough. Slavery has demanded more; and, when we refused to grant more, she seized her wicked bludgeon, and tried to demolish the fabric of that fair Union which had sheltered her treasonable head. Now let her have what she has invoked. Let it be war to the death. Let the monstrous Aggressor find no shelter, henceforth, under the flag she has profaned and betrayed.

I rejoice that the time has come, at last, when a man may characterize this odious outrage upon humanity, in the language it merits, and have all his brethren say, Amen. All political controversies, in this land, have become narrowed to a single point: Do you love Slavery?—Yes, or No? If you love it, then you love the mortal enemy of this Government, of Civilization, and of Christianity; and if you are not a traitor, you avow yourself the friend of the Arch-Traitor, and the difference is not worth sticking for. On the other hand, if you don't love Slavery, you hate it; and, hating it, you cordially support the Press, the Platform, and the Pulpit, that are now locking hands to exterminate it. Thus, all former distinctions disappear, and all good men coalesce in one great Party,—the party of Patriotism, of Civilization, and of Religion. Who is it that stands outside the Ring, with the assassins of Baltimore; and the piratical Crew that have conspired to burn our free cities, and murder our Chief Magistrate? There are none left. We are all in the ranks of Liberty—a brotherhood of Patriots and Christians—with the noblest banner on earth waving over us. In past times, I have been among those who suffered some inconvenience by speaking against the great Despotism; but I never murmured at the temporary disapprobation under which I stood, for I saw that the fullness of time had almost come, when the sternest opponent of Slavery would be justified by all men. That day is now at hand, and my grateful heart glows in its beams. True, I regret that this consummation was not effected by peaceful means; but we must accept what God appoints; and since war is the instrument of our deliverance, I accept the war. I accept anything rather than a return to that servility of spirit, that allowed Slavery to lord it over the heritage of freemen.

I compassionate the Southern people, so hopelessly involved in the swift-footed vengeance that must sweep their land. They are not, radically, more guilty than ourselves; only the diabolical system that has possessed them so long, has inoculated many of them with its own malignity. I feel like making great allowance for the bad schooling those people have suffered from. So deplorably has Slavery enervated their moral principles, and darkened their sense of right, that they no longer realize either what they do, or what they are. They are the saddest victims of their own oppression. They are like drunkards, besotted by their cups, and madly clinging to the terrible vice that has ruined them. O! for their sake—even more than for our own—let us swear eternal hostility to the system that has perverted a noble people, and turned a fruitful land into a howling desert. True, we must draw the sword against them,—for their salvation and ours, we must appeal to the God of battles,—but, as Heaven is our witness, Compassion shall temper the warfare they have provoked; and our vengeance fall, only, upon that .villainous despotism, which has brought discord between us.

II.

WAR AND PEACE:

THE REAL CAUSE—THE FINAL REMEDY.*

But the Wisdom that is from above, is first pure, then peaceable.—JAMES iii, 17.

I shall speak, this morning, of the Conditions and Securities of Peace. The topic is seasonable and important. In no experience of mine, has it ever assumed such magnitude. Under a social convulsion that shakes the Republic, from its marble Capitol to the rudest cabin on the frontier,—under the turbulent emotions that pervade even our churches and our homes,—under the great emergency that has flowered out, in this calm May season, in martial banners, in the tramp of stern brigades, and in the crimson panoply of War,—who does not recall, with a poignant regret, the blessed days of concord and peace?

We are not a people who love dissension, or who profit by violence. We love PEACE; and we have shown ourselves willing, more than once, to make sacrifices in order to secure it. Our taste, our temper, and our interest agree in this. We have not been quick to fire at an insult, and ready to avenge a wrong with a blow. We have not boasted that our honor was tender, or bragged that our valor could paralize the world. We have had little to say about being a "chivalrous" people; though we have tried to pay our debts, to educate our children, and make our surroundings tidy and respectable. We have been patient and diligent—anxious to avoid unpleasant subjects, and willing, for the most part, to mind our own business. Our

---

* This discourse was not written out in full. I cannot, therefore, re-produce the entire language employed in its delivery.

3

grievances we have handed over to the professional politicians, that they might fight them out, on the platform and in Congress, with as little scandal and loss of time as possible. So thoroughly has the love of peace possessed us,—I mean the great body of the people of the Free States,—that martial exercises had degenerated into farces and holidays; the soldier had become a mere *actor* to the sanguine speculators in human progress; and the great armories and navy yards were regarded as relics of Barbarism. And yet—with all this love of peace—with all our solicitude to guard it and perpetuate it—with all our confident persuasion that the millennium of peace would remain unbroken,—here we are, all at once, plunged to the neck in War.

Who is to blame for this dire catastrophe? Some charge the crime upon the Abolitionists; some, upon the disappointed demagogues of the South; some, upon the Republican Party, and others, upon the Ministers. I think the real responsibility rests with neither. The true source of the disorder is to be sought elsewhere, as I shall presently attempt to show.

While the Nation has been falling into war, some of the Churches have been equally unfortunate. The catastrophe has been equally unforeseen—equally unprovoked—in the churches and in the nation. For, if our fellow-citizens have been friends of peace, and solicitous to secure and perpetuate the genial blessing, the same may be said of our church people. How often have they said, with David, " Behold how good, and how pleasant a thing it is, for brethren to dwell together in unity." On the score of enjoyment, and of temporary interest, at least, how ardently is peace to be desired. Members of churches have always felt this, and they have felt that many things might be safely sacrificed in order to promote concord. The Clergy have had even stronger motives to preserve, by every means in their power, unity and peace among their members; for their pecuniary interest, their tranquility of mind, and their temporary reputation,.have all been involved in it. There can be little doubt—reflecting on the average temper of human nature, and on the real situation of the Clergy—that most of them have suppressed some of their convictions, and softened the severity of many a rebuke as it rushed to their lips for utterance—from a dread of wounding somebody's feelings, or alienating somebody's patronage—and thereby giving occasion for turbulence and complaint. If those people who have taken offence at what the preacher has actually spoken,—(believing that he has wantonly wounded them,)—could know how much more he has withheld, out of regard to their feelings, they would, perhaps, mitigate their censure.

And yet, with all our anxiety to preserve peace in the churches, peace has not been preserved. With all our sacrifices, with all our forbearance, discord has broken in. With whom, or with what, rests the responsibility? I shall try to show where the fault lies. This will lead me to exhibit—as I proposed, in the beginning—the Conditions and Securities of Peace.

If you were to enclose two bands of men in a tropical garden—nay, in Paradise, if you please—whose characters, tastes, interests, and ambitions were absolutely opposite, do you think it would be a peaceable community? One band lives by robbery; the other, by industry. One is lawless and profligate, domineering and aggressive; the other is diligent and decorous, thoughtful and just. What one admires, the other holds in contempt; and what one abhors, the other loves. With feelings, interests, and pursuits in radical conflict, how could they share the same province, in peace? Grant that their domain contains bread enough for both,—grant that the dew and rain fall upon both alike,—and grant that some preacher stands among them, entreating them to love each other. Do you think that all this would avail to make a peaceable community, where the radical elements of character, the desires and impulses of the two parties, were diametrically repugnant? I tell you nay: there can be no real concord between things essentially evil and things essentially good.

Now, the American Republic is that Paradise we have supposed. Slave Society and Free Society are the two bands that possess it together. Their characters and tendencies, their

aims and desires, are completely hostile. Slave Society rests
upon robbery—for it holds by force, what it has no claim to
hold in equity; asserting that claim of property in man which
is repugnant to natural justice. Free Society rests upon the
voluntary industry of the people, and is guarded by equity.
Slave Society tyrannizes over the weak; Free Society extends
over the weak, the protection of Law. Slave Society makes
brute force supreme; Free Society makes Justice supreme.
In Slave Society, a handful of aristocrats govern the State,
and the masses of the inhabitants are disregarded like cattle.
In Free Society, political power is distributed among all the
people; and the most vigorous thinker is the mightiest man.
In Slave Society, everything is at the mercy of an unthinking
and capricious Despotism, and the tendency of community is
irretrievably downward; but, in Free Society, great questions
are settled by discussion, by reflection, by reason;—every
man's interest is safe, because natural justice is revered, and
everything is open to investigation;—and so the community is
continually being elevated, and fortified by the private conscience and public intelligence.

Such are the two hostile interests that have been subsisting
in this Republic, from the beginning. Our fathers—with many
scruples and doubts—set them up housekeeping, in the same
edifice, because they supposed that Slave Society would soon
die a natural death, and they were scarcely prepared to kill it
by violent means. For eighty years, these two types of Society
have been developing in the Nation,—each according to its
nature,—each obedient to its own instinct. In the exact ratio
of their growth, has been their aggression upon each other.
When the house began to resound with their strife, all the
peace-makers turned out to settle the quarrel. The more they
tried to settle it, the more fiercely the quarrel raged; and, step
by step, by a series of ineffectual compromises that only irritated
what they were expected to heal, we have journeyed on to
Civil War.

Now, there are men, I dare say, who will never cease to
marvel at the perverse obstinacy of the American people, in

keeping up agitation. Why could'nt they let Slavery alone? Why could'nt Slavery let them alone? Why could'nt we have had peace? Why has no power been given us to put down this everlasting nigger question? Why won't men let it alone? and why, of all other men, won't our minister let it alone? The mystery is, doubtless, very great; but shall we not make an attempt, this pleasant morning, to look into it, and gain at least a clue to the reason?

Suppose you plant Canada thistles on one side of your garden, and a bed of strawberry plants on the opposite side, and charge them not to meddle with each other! You will soon find that they will meddle with each other—not because they are willful, but because each must obey the law of its own nature. Now Slave Society and Free Society have their peculiar instincts, and each develops agreeably to its own law. They must encroach upon each other, they must conflict, they must quarrel; and, what God and Nature have thus made hostile, we cannot join together in harmony.

Slave Society imbues those who grow up under its spirit, with a despotic and lawless disposition. Free Society imbues people with a sense of justice, liberalizes and elevates the mind, and prepares the heart to feel the liveliest sympathy for the weak and the oppressed. Thus, the tendencies of the two systems—by their legitimate operation—involve collision and strife. How can we help ourselves? Can the man who was nourished at the breast of Despotism, be otherwise than tyrannical? Can the offspring of Liberty disown his mother, or resist the generous impulses that spring from his blood? We must all have noticed how vain it is, to attempt to override or suppress an hereditary trait; and these instincts that are born with us, and fostered by the society in which we are reared, cannot be controlled by any arbitrary edict. We may as well make up our minds to face the fact, first as last: There will be no peace—at best, only a short truce—while these belligerents occupy the same house. We need a public opinion, in America, that shall recognize this Fact, for this is the first condition of Peace.

We have all railed, more or less, at the ultra men of the South—at the "fire-eaters," as they have been named;—but we might as well rail at the Canada thistles, when they manifest a desire to monopolize the garden. They are obeying the instincts of Slave Society; and your entreaties and expostulations—as the event has repeatedly proved—might as well have been addressed to thistles as to that class of men.

Suppose a company of Indian Thugs come into the neighborhood, buy a certain amount of real estate, and settle among us. It is the profession of the Thug to murder; and, in him, the tendency to murder has the force of an instinct. Murders are perpetrated; the community is in arms; and the Thugs are disposed of agreeably to law and equity. But, however heinous the crime, it was no greater than was to have been expected, in view of the habits of the Thugs. So with Slave Society. All its habitudes and instincts are aggressive and destructive. Don't abuse my metaphor, and misapprehend my idea. I am not denying that individual slave-holders may be very fair men. Some natures are proof against the worst social influences. I speak of the system of Slavery, in its essence and general effects. And I say, without the fear of my position being successfully controverted, that the most odious developments of Southern Society are the legitimate outgrowths of Slavery,—things which it is idle to protest against, so long as we foster the seed that produces them.

We have complained, also, against the ultra Anti-Slavery men. But, candidly and philosophically viewed, what have they done but obey the instincts of Free Society? It was just as natural for Free Society to develop the Abolitionist party, as it was for your strawberry bed to throw out "runners" toward the Canada thistles. How futile it is to quarrel with any such settled tendency of nature. How unwise it is to ignore such facts, instead of accommodating ourselves to them! We might as reasonably attempt to resist gravitation, or any other natural law, as attempt to carry out a peace policy, in violation of these immutable conditions.

Free Society fills every bosom, that is open to its influences, with the love of free institutions—with the love of justice, mercy, and manhood;—and it inspires us, at the same time, with an irrepressible abhorrence of the injustice, the profligacy, and the ignorance which are the fruits of Slavery. Under this influence, it is impossible that men should hold their peace. The full heart will make its emotions audible in burning words. Almost involuntarily—almost against a man's will—he thunders out his hatred of tyranny, and chants the hymns of Freedom. It is the Holy Spirit of God that impels his utterance; and Timidity and Compromise have no padlocks strong enough to shut the mouth of a live man, when the trumpet sounds and the Hour has come.

Thus far, I have tried to show the true conditions of Peace, from the nature of the two interests that are warring with each other, in this country. I shall now proceed to show that the preceding view is confirmed by the principle brought to view in the text: "The wisdom that is from above, is first pure, then peaceable."

Consider, then, how obvious it is, as a general fact, that, when a conflict takes place, in society, between the good elements and the bad, there can be no permanent peace, until the bad elements are eradicated. A bad principle in the social system, is like a disease in the human system;—it is a source of irritation and unrest, to the whole body politic. The patient is in ceaseless pain, apprehension, and depression; and, even when he affects to rest, he moans, and tosses his limbs about, and starts as from ghastly dreams. How will you restore the man to his natural tranquility, and to the enjoyment of his existence? Will you sit at his bed, and sing a lullaby? Will you expatiate on the blessings of rest? Will you remind him how commendable it is to be quiet and serene? Or, will you endeavor to expel the man's disease, and ensure him tranquility, by first endowing him with health?

My brethren, that patient is our Country. If you would not mock the misery of a man, by affecting to lull him to rest while his malady rendered rest impossible—why will you mock the agony of our country, by singing lullabys, and ignoring the distemper that brings all the pain? American Society has always had in its blood one virulent distemper. That distemper has been the source of all our trouble, agitation, discord and danger; and now it has assumed an alarming phase. It has broken out in the ghastly form of treason. Now, what does the Crisis require, at the hands of reasonable and faithful men? What can it require, but the radical cure of the Patient? Purify the social system, and the American Republic will have peace. This is the inflexible logic of the hour, in my estimation, and all remedies that come short of it, will only betray us into deeper misfortune.

If you ask by what means Slavery is to be abolished, in this country, I must say, that I am not competent to inform you. But, coming events will declare them. God will show us the means, as the great controversy goes forward. Let there be a will, and there will be a way opened. The course of Righteousness is never impeded, except by human prejudice and fear. Meantime, I hold it the patriot's first duty,—next to the rescue of our soil from Rebellion,—to exert himself to create a right public sentiment, in relation to the final disposal of Slavery. The great question will come before the American people—sooner, perhaps, than we apprehend; and it is of the first importance that we be prepared to meet it, in the true spirit of Christianity, of Reason, of Philosophy and of Justice. And I appeal to all my brethren and fellow citizens—whether, in time past, we have not been too devoted to the interests of partizanship, and too negligent of the claims of our Country,—whether we have not been too jealous of having Religion approach the province of Politics,—whether we do not now obviously need the light of the heavenly wisdom to reveal the path of duty,—and whether the hour has not come for men of honor and intelligence, to put away all the prejudices and jealousies that have hitherto blinded them; while they bring all the gifts of their nature together, and offer them—as an oblation to God—on the altar of Christian Patriotism.

I have spoken these words in the interests of Peace; and because I know that no peace is possible except by apprehending the real cause of the disturbance, and manfully putting it away. I love peace so well—I prize it so highly—that I will do what I can to secure a substantial peace, and not a mere deceptive truce. This Slavery agitation has not only been the bane of the Nation, but the sorrow of the Church, these many years; but there is no hope of getting rid of the agitation, so long as the exciting cause continues to exist. For the sake of every interest that is dear to us, as Patriots and as Christians,—for the sake of social tranquility and brotherly love,—let us unite to put down the great offence. For my own part, I am willing to incur temporary censure, and to suffer temporary loss, if I can contribute anything to the formation of a public sentiment that shall restore true peace to this Country, by renovating the social system.

THE CLERGY:

THE RELATION OF THE PULPIT TO SLAVERY.

———— ✢ ————

"Come now and let us reason together, saith the Lord."—Isaiah i, 18.

The faculty of reason is the crowning glory of our nature. By virtue of it, men are capable of immeasurable improvement. It is the bond between them and superior beings. It is the great attribute—common to God and man—by which the Divine Being communicates his will; establishes intercourse with his creatures, and sways over them a moral government. Reason is, to a human being, just what a rudder is to a ship,—it is the means by which God steers him in the direction of the moral law.

There is always hope of people who are susceptible of being reasoned with. The better argument, the nobler influence, sways them. The evidence from without, is justified by the tribunal within, and they say, "This is conclusive; this is enough." It is only the people who can not, or will not, *reason*, who baffle us to the last; and who—hearing neither Moses nor the prophets—would not be persuaded though one should rise from the dead. As Henry More quaintly observes: "When a man is so fugitive and unsettled that he will not stand to the verdict of his own Faculties, one can no more fasten anything upon him, than he can write in the water, or tie knots of the wind."

As God has no higher influence to exert than the influence of reason, He can delegate none more potent to His servants.

The ministers of His kingdom are authorized to reason with mankind; and they are bound to reason faithfully, kindly, persistently. But the result must be left to the Searcher of the hearts, and the Judge of all motives.

It is our lot to live in eventful days, and to participate in momentous controversies. It is our fortune to be troubled and tried. It is our fate to be divided and shaken. Every man must be responsible for his own actions, and God shall be the Judge between us. It is the lot of the Clergy of the Free States to differ, widely, from part of their congregations, on the subject of ministerial duty. It is their fate to incur, on account of this difference, no little censure and opposition. I have called this congregation together, this evening, for the purpose of reasoning with those who object to the position taken by the clergy, in their occasional discussion of national affairs.

1. In the first place, let us group together three or four significant facts :

First—The Clergy of the Free States, with few exceptions, hold the same views concerning American Slavery. Divided into various sects, arrayed under hostile denominational banners, and rivals in ecclesiastical influence, they are substantially united in their estimate of Slavery, and of the treatment it should receive at the hands of a Christian people. Such unanimity of opinion probably never before characterized a body of intelligent men, so variously trained, and differing so widely on other questions.

Second—What is the fair and natural inference to be drawn from this fact? Have these men entered into a conspiracy to hold and propagate particular sentiments? This can not be the case, for there is scarcely any intercourse between them, beyond their denominational lines; and they are too much estranged by sectarian jealousy to have come into any premeditated concert of action. Have they any personal interest to subserve, by taking an attitude hostile to Slavery, or by favoring the ascendency of a particular party? This can hardly be; for they seek no office in the gift of any party, and

28   THE RELATIONS OF SLAVERY TO THE WAR.

they covet no spoils consequent upon a partizan triumph. If
there be a class of men in this land, above the suspicion of
being actuated by mercenary motives, in their political action,
or in their strictures upon public measures, it is the Clergy.
As a class, they live by the favors of no party, but they are
independent of all parties. Their private interest is in no
way affected by the vicissitudes of parties; and whether their
influence is cast in favor of a particular party, or against it, it
is not cast in the interest of selfishness. Some of the Clergy
have, indeed, spoken to the prejudice of their pockets and of
their peace; but no man can convict them of having been
actuated by a sordid motive, in trying to awaken the public
conscience to the iniquities of Pro-Slavery politics.

If the Clergy have thus imbibed strong Anti-Slavery convictions, without concert or mutual understanding,—and if
they are now proclaiming these convictions, independently of
any private motives, and, in many instances, against their personal interest,—what is the reasonable inference? The inference is, that they are, at least, sincere in their convictions, and
honorable in their purposes. Are they, then, so ignorant, or
so imbecile, as to be *disqualified* for holding a weighty opinion
on questions involving the well-being of their country? If so,
it is remarkable that they should be located among the learned
Professions, and referred to, in the familiar language of Society,
as Teachers. What, TEACHERS!—and not qualified to decide
whether the discussion of Slavery comes, or does not come,
within the province of the Pulpit? TEACHERS!—and not
qualified to state the simple facts concerning the history of the
system, the relations of the Church thereto, and the estimate
formed of it by Christians and Patriots, in the different ages
and departments of Christendom? TEACHERS!—and yet *con-
tradicted* by hot-headed party men, who do not even claim
extended information, and who derive their opinions from fifth-
rate newspapers, notoriously conducted in the interests of
partizanship? I ask you all, as men responsible for your sentiments and your actions, what is the reasonable inference from
these things?

Third—Not only are nearly all the Clergy of the Free States, in all denominations, in agreement as regards the subject of Slavery, but an immense majority of the *people* of these States, manifest a similar unanimity of sentiment. This has not always been the fact; but it has come to be. A deliberate observation of the effects of Slavery in American Society,—a prolonged experience of the tendency of the system to demoralize our politics,—have brought almost all the intelligent people of the Free States, as well as a respectable minority in the Slave States, to the belief, that Slavery is not only wrong in the abstract, but a pernicious and dangerous thing to foster.

Fourth—With the Clergy, and this large majority of the American people, all Christian nations agree. The public opinion of Europe is about unanimous in condemnation of Slavery; the last vestige of the system is just now disappearing, in Russia; and there is not a man, among the great nationalities of the East, eminent for either learning, patriotism, or piety, who would dishonor himself far enough to become its advocate.

II. So much for Facts. Now I ask, what conclusion a reasoning mind must naturally draw from them? That the Clergy are in the way of their duty, or out of it, in the hostile attitude they occupy toward Slavery?

Here are two great Armies being joined in conflict: On one side, Freedom—on the other, Despotism. On the side of Freedom, are Civilization, with all the Arts that have embellished the world,—Learning, that has opened illimitable fields to the mind of man,—and the Christian Religion, that has refined our social life and sanctified our homes, while revealing, beyond this clouded isle of Care and Trouble, a sweet celestial shore. On the side of Despotism, is brutal Ignorance, hand-locked with debasing Superstition. She is marshaled on by ruffianly violence, with Law and Justice trampled under her feet. Behind her, are Desolation and Mourning, and the long perspective of Barbarism.

Such are the two parties now arrayed in hostile lines. Can you doubt which side the Clergy must espouse? Can you

wonder at the choice they have made? As friends of their
Country,—as champions of their race,—as teachers of their
Religion,—how could they hesitate? Do you claim that they
should not commit themselves,—that they should be indifferent
to the great decision now impending? Then God should take
the souls out of their bosoms, and give them an oyster's life,
in place of the immortal love of liberty He has kindled there;
for, constituted as we are, it is impossible to be indifferent
when swords are to be crossed in the name of our Country's
fame and freedom. But they will divide their congregations.
This is to be lamented. But it is no excuse for silence. A minister better divide the spirit from the body, than be dumb as a
clam, at such an hour as this. There is nothing a minister can
suffer from, half so calamitous as the loss of self-respect; for
that is the mainspring of whatever power there may be in the
man. It is unpleasant to be misjudged and traduced; but, to
be a conscious poltroon is to forfeit every claim to the confidence of community.

If a minister will be a faithful Leader, and not a ductile
dough-face, he will be in advance of some of his people. He
will break ground that is not familiar—not already tracked
over by the feet of the multitude. It is his business, as a
Teacher, to keep on the frontier of Public Opinion,—to be
governed by the facts that have come to his knowledge, and
not by the irrational prejudices that time has refuted, and that
he can no longer respect. It is his business, as the Friend of
his Church and as the Servant of Mankind, to keep abreast of
the best thought that is moving through Society,—to keep in
the van of Christian Civilization ; and he should not be expected
to tack and drift, because some of his people—not looking from
his stand-point—think that he has transcended his province.
Such things should neither change his purpose, nor perturb
his spirit; but he should say, "I'm sorry, brethren, we're not
to sail together any longer; but, since you insist on paddling
out of the fleet, you shall go with our blessing. WE must
sail by the Chart; and we can't alter the course of the flag-
ship, for the sake of keeping you in the squadron."

III. A minority of our people have contracted the habit of declaring, that "a minister has no business to meddle with Slavery." There are a few persons, holding this opinion, whom I sincerely esteem, and I desire to reason with them on the question. It is possible that I shall present considerations which have not occurred to them, and which will tend to place the subject in a different light. In the first place, in affirming that "a minister has no business to preach against Slavery," you assume to know, better than he does, what his business really is. I think you are bound to show how you come to be so much better informed than I am, on a subject to which I have given my chief attention, but which lies outside of your own calling.

When you employ a lawyer to conduct a cause, do you undertake to instruct him how to extract his testimony, or how to make his plea? Or, do you concede that he is the best judge of his own business; and that any interference on your part would be both a reflection on his intelligence, and a damage to your interest? When you call a physician to minister to your malady, do you, at the same time, profess to understand the case better than he does, or offer to dictate what remedies shall be employed? If you actually supposed yourself wiser than the physician, you would not send for him at all.

Now you employ a man to stand in the pulpit, as a Teacher of the Christian Religion, and of the moral obligations of mankind. In engaging him to teach, you are supposed to believe him qualified to teach. You believe him qualified, because he has made Religion and Morals his special study. You have, yourself, general impressions and convictions on those subjects, (as you have general impressions and convictions in relation to Law and medicine,) but you have not qualified yourself to be a Teacher of one, more than of the other. And yet—(now mark your inconsistency.)—when that man, whom you have placed in the pulpit expressly to teach, happens to offend some of your prejudices, you tell him that he has made a mistake,— that he has no business to say such and such things,—and sometimes you even deny matters of fact, merely because they had not come to your knowledge. By this course, you reverse the relations of the parties; for, whereas you promoted me awhile ago to be your Teacher, in relation to the specific subject which I had made my life study, you are now assuming to be mine. But, the worst phase of your censure is, that you assume to know my duty better than I know it myself, which is an aggression upon my personal liberty, to which I can submit on no account.

Why has a minister no business to preach against Slavery? It is universally assumed, and believed, that it is his business to expose every form of sin; and, by making it odious and repugnant,—and by exhibiting its destructive consequences,—persuade mankind to put it away. Among the sins of the world, what rank does Slavery occupy? This can be determined, only, by reflecting what Slavery is—in its essence and in its effects.

"Slavery," is defined by Webster, as "a state of entire subjection to the will of another." "A Slave," says the Code of Louisiana, "is in the power of the master to whom he belongs. The master may sell him, dispose of his person, his industry, his labor; he can do nothing, possess nothing, nor acquire anything, but which must belong to his master." In the language of the Laws of South Carolina, "Slaves shall be deemed, taken, reputed, and adjudged to be chattels personal in the hands of their masters, and possessions to all intents and purposes whatsoever."

Under the mildest form, then, Slavery asserts an absolute ownership in man. That is, under Slavery, one human being may own another human being, in the same sense in which you own a horse or a dog. The slave's person is absolutely at the master's disposal,—the slave's labor, virtue, and will, are in the master's power,—just as the body of any brute, which you may own, is in your power. Now, in asserting this absolute claim of ownership in human beings, Slavery usurps the prerogative of the Almighty. "All souls are mine, saith the Lord." Since all men belong to God, no man can belong to his brother man.

God gave man dominion over the beasts of the field, the fowl of the air, and the fish of the sea, but not over his own image; and any claim of property in man, is unlawful and impious:— unlawful, because not authorized by the Divine Statute, and impious, because a flagrant invasion of God's peculiar prerogative. Thus, Slavery is a great wrong, in its very essence. Even where the master is kind, and where the servitude is mild, the slave is wronged in this : that his manhood is ignored, and he is ranked with cattle; and that none of the thoughts, privileges or rights, natural to a human being, are secured to him. The man who is kind to his horse or his dog, will probably be kind to his slave; but, the very fact that the slave is degraded to the level of the horse and dog, constitutes the moral indignity which our Religion sternly rebukes.

Remember, then, that Slavery is wrong, in its very essence— in every conceivable instance. In the next place, consider what an outrage it becomes where the master is cruel, licentious, depraved. It is not necessary to suppose slave-holders any worse, by nature, than other men; though no reflecting person can fail to see that the effects of the system are exceedingly demoralizing. It cannot be denied that those who are abusive or cruel to their brute property, must be at least equally so to men and women, who, like the brutes, are absolutely in their power. The master who is arbitrary and capricious, profligate and violent, has a power over the person of the slave, that is little short of infernal. I do not speak of blows from the lash, or rigorous service in the field, mitigated by no reward and cheered by no hope. The slave so circumstanced, is exposed to worse indignities. The honor of man has no defense. The modesty of woman has no refuge. The best instincts of human nature are brutally violated. Not one of the domestic sanctities, or relations, is secure from despotic and lawless outrage. We may try to flatter ourselves that such instances are rare. Unhappily, they are frequent. Nor is it so much the fault of the slave-holder as it is the necessary consequence of the system of Slavery, which disarms the weak,

5

incites the strong, and offers both the temptation to outrage, and boundless opportunity to satiate the worst passions.

Let any man reflect what human nature is, among the average men of the South, or even of the North; let him reflect that those men are the absolute masters of other men, of women, and of children; let him remember that the slaves have no defense against the avarice, the lust, or the cruelty of their masters—and how can he fail to see that the system offers every invitation to outrage, and that it involves, as its daily consequence, the blackest sins against which the law of God is arrayed?

If we look at the social results of Slavery, as developed in the civilization of the South, we see that the fruit is consistent with the seed. All good influences retire before the scourge. Education is discouraged. Liberty of speech is denied. Enterprize withers, and even the soil becomes sterile. The Church, poisoned by the baneful social atmosphere, mutters delirious sophistry, and becomes the pimp of the slave-holder. Presently—all the vigorous timbers of Society having rotted away—the foundations of social order break up. Entire States slump into Barbarism. Anarchy comes up, with mobs for its authority, and with Treason for its watch-word. It is the last result of Slavery—private licentiousness reaching out to demoralize communities—the despotism of the private Plantation raving to assert itself in the Capitol of the Nation. It is the great scarlet Abomination culminating in maturest bloom.

Such is Slavery—a system combining, in its essence and in its results, a greater volume of Iniquity than can be found under any other name. Yet, we are told that a Christian minister has no business to meddle with it! God says to the minister, " Cry aloud and spare not: lift up thy voice, like a trumpet, and show my people their sins!" But, some of the congregation say, " Nay; there be sins among us which the minister is not to expose: He must be silent concerning our great national Iniquity, lest people accuse him of ' preaching politics,' and he break up the Church!" That is to say, the minister may denounce those sins that are like mole-hills—and

especially those antiquated sins that have ceased to be prac-
ticed; but, before this great Malakoff of Iniquity, that threatens
to desolate a hemisphere, he must be dumb. In other words,
a Christian Church, organized expressly to make war upon all
sin, is in danger of going to pieces, if the pastor offers to wake
up the the public conscience in relation to the most notorious,
and most dangerous sin, now thriving in this world!

I have not alluded to the most abhorrent features disclosed in
the practical operation of Slavery. I have said nothing of the
necessary reaction of the system, in demoralizing white fami-
lies—in corrupting the youth, in destroying female delicacy,
and thus tainting, at the domestic fountain, the moral life of
Society. I have not alluded to the disgusting exhibitions of
immodesty and brutality, that are presented in the slave-mar-
kets ; exhibitions that degrade the nominally Christian cities
of New Orleans, Savannah and Charleston, to the level of
Constantinople. Nor have I said anything of those well-
authenticated cases, in which the enormity of Slavery culmi-
nates in a union of lust and avarice, that outrages brutehood
as much as it shames humanity,—cases in which the master
becomes bound to his slave by the closest tie of nature, and
sells his own child into perdition, as he would sell a calf to the
butcher!

These are the incidental and natural effects of Slavery.
They are the notorious fruits of the system. If there are
any persons among us ignorant of the facts, or disposed to
question them, they have neither reflected on the nature of
Slavery, nor availed themselves of information accessible to
any person disposed to investigate the subject. Such, I repeat,
are the nature and effects of Slavery; and yet, it has been
said, that a preacher has no business to lift up his voice against
this colossal sin! If it is not his proper work to expose this
unspeakable outrage, I beg to know what his proper work is.
It has been said, that the stability of our Churches would be
periled, if preachers persisted in exposing Slavery to the condemnation of the Divine law! Is it meant by this, that there
are men in the Churches, who will support them only on con-

dition that ministers remain blind and dumb before this intolerable wrong? Is it meant that the Churches have become, in some sense, allies of the slave-holder—since, by exposing *his* sins, we rupture *their* unity?

IV. Having now shown that Slavery is of such a wicked and destructive nature, that ministers must assail it, in the name of their Religion, if they are obligated to assail any sin whatsoever—I proceed to show that the position of the Clergy is fortified by the general sentiment of Christendom, as expressed by Theologians, by Jurists, and by Statesmen.

Lactantius, who was tutor to the son of Constantine, " was faithful in his denunciation of Slavery, and reckoned the work of redeeming captives and slaves the most divine of human employments."

St. Cyprian, an eminent Christian martyr of the Second Century, says, in his Address to the Bishops of Numedia, " Both religion and morality make it a duty for us to work for the deliverance of the captives. They are sanctuaries of Jesus Christ, who have fallen into the hands of the Infidel. It is Jesus himself whom we ought to consider in our captive brothers; it is Him whom we should deliver from captivity— Him who has delivered us from death." In his Treatise against Demetrius, he uses the following severe language: " You expect from your slave that he be devoted to you, man of a day. Is this slave less a man than you? He came into the world on the same conditions,—your equal by his birth, by his death,—provided with the same organs; endowed, as well as you, with a reasoning soul; called to the same hopes; subject to the same laws, as well for the present life, as for the time to come. You oblige him to obey you and be subject to you; and, if he happen to forget for one moment the right you have to command him,—if he neglect to execute your orders with a rigorous precision,—misfortune to him! . . . Miserable man! While you know so well how to maintain your quality of master over a man, you are not willing to recognize the Master and Lord of all men!"

St. Ambrose, who lived in the Third Century, held similar sentiments; and he ordered that priests should sell, if necessary, even the sacred vases of the Churches, to redeem slaves. How different the feelings of that great Prelate from the policy of those who would close a minister's lips against any condemnation of Slavery, for the sake of retaining a few dollars in the treasury of the Church !

When Louis X, in 1315, enfranchised all the serfs belonging to the Crown, he made the noble declaration that " Slavery is contrary to nature, which intended that all men by birth should be free and equal ; that, since his Kingdom was denominated the Kingdom of the Franks, or Freemen, it appeared just and right that the fact should correspond with the name."

As early as the Fifth Century, Slavery was condemned from the chair of St. Peter. Pope Paul III " imprecated a curse on those Europeans who should enslave Indians, or any other class of men." Leo the Xth, declared that " not the Christian religion only, but nature herself cries out against the state of Slavery." " In 1102, St. Anselm held a national council in St. Peter's Church, at Westminster, in which, a canon of the council prescribed—" Let no one, henceforth, presume to carry on the wicked traffic, by which men in England have hitherto been sold like brute animals."

Wycliffe, who has been called " the morning star of the Reformation," asserted " that it was contrary to the principles of the Christian religion, that any one should be a slave." Coming down to our own country, we find the sentiments of the great Christian leaders the same, as regards this subject. Whitfield and Edwards, the champions of Calvanism ; Wesley, the father of Methodism ; Winchester, the Universalist, and Channing, the Unitarian, were all bold in their denunciations of Slavery.

Such has been the feeling, and such the practice, of the Christian Church, in all its branches and in all ages ; and yet, in opposition to this " cloud of witnesses "—absolutely filling the horizon of Christian History—men now undertake to maintain, that a minister deviates from his legitimate calling in exposing this wicked system. The truth is, that he deviates from his true calling, only, when he is persuaded to let the subject alone. Then, all the faithful standard-bearers of Christianity, who have maintained the cause of Freedom, in past ages, through good and evil report, rise up in judgment against the timid time-server, who denies his Lord by forsaking those who are in bonds!

But I must hasten on, and show you how Slavery is regarded by the jurisprudence of Christendom. Sir William Blackstone, who remains to this day, I believe, one of the best authorities in the legal profession, holds the following language: "The law that supports Slavery, must necessarily be condemned as cruel; for every feeling of human nature advocates liberty. Slavery is introduced through human wickedness; but God advocates liberty by the nature he has given to man. In popular language, we speak of good laws, and bad laws. The Bible, which generally uses the popular language, speaks of 'mischief framed by a law.' It remains true—strictly and philosophically speaking—there is no law contrary to equity."

In this doctrine, all the British Judges of eminence, are believed to have concurred—excepting only the infamous Jeffreys, whose dissent, considering the character of the man, really lends weight to the opinions of such jurists as Blackstone, Mansfield, and Chesterfield.

The estimate of Slavery, made by our own most illustrious statesmen, is well known, already. I will detain you long enough to quote the testimony of a few of them, by way of completing the argument. Almost all the leading men of the revolutionary period, have left us the testimony of their hostility to Slavery. Governeur Morris declared before the Constitutional Convention—"I never will concur in upholding domestic Slavery. It is a nefarious Institution. It is the curse of Heaven." William Pinckney characterized Slavery as "iniquitous and most dishonorable; founded in a disgraceful traffic; as shameful in its continuance as in its origin." He adds that, "by the eternal principles of natural justice, no master has a right to hold his slave in bondage a single hour."

John Jay, the first Chief Justice of the United States, stigmatized Slavery as " a sin of crimson dye." Patrick Henry, the orator of the Revolution, said: "I will not—I cannot justify it." Four of the early Presidents have recorded their testimony against Slavery. Washington said, that it was " among his first wishes to see some plan adopted by which Slavery might be abolished by law ; and that for this purpose, his suffrage should not be wanting." John Adams declared that, " consenting to Slavery is a sacrilegious breach of trust." Madison believed it " wrong to admit in the Constitution, the idea of property in man." But Jefferson excels all his contemporaries in the amplitude of his testimony on the subject. He declared his belief that "the day is not distant when the public mind of this country must bear and adopt the proposisition for emancipation, or worse will follow ;" and that " if something is not done, and soon done, we shall be the murderers of our own children." He characterizes Slavery as " a hideous blot,"—as " a bondage, one hour of which, is fraught with more misery than ages of that which the people of this country rose in rebellion to oppose." In the latest of his published letters, he says : " My sentiments on the subject of Negro Slavery, have long since been in possession of the public, and time has only served to give them stronger root. The love of justice and the love of country plead equally the cause of these people ; and it is a mortal reproach to us, that they should have pleaded it so long in vain."

I have thus tried to lay the subject of Slavery before you, so that you may see the essence of the system, its pernicious effects, and the light in which it has been regarded by the best minds in Christendom, throughout all ages. No person, who has attended me through the discussion, can fail to see the obligation resting upon a minister of Christ, to expose and resist this monstrous iniquity. If the Gospel of Christ is hostile to any sin, it is hostile to this. If the Clergy have authority to rebuke any wrong, they are obligated to face the system of Slavery with their sternest indignation.

Especially urgent, at this time, are the claims of Patriotism
and Liberty upon the American Clergy. You have sent your
young men to the field, to vindicate your country's honor.
You have declared that it is every man's duty to do the best
he can, in his own province, to aid his country, in this hour of
its peril. Shall the Clergy of this land do nothing? only
mutter abstractions that nobody now hears or heeds? Is there
nothing ministers can do to aid the holy cause that fills every
man's bosom? If there be anything, what is it? They have
their function, at this time, as you have yours. As soldiers of
Jesus Christ, let them be as bold and faithful as the men you
have sent to the tented field. Let them bring the Divine Wisdom—which they are authorized to administer—to interpret
the problem of the times. Let them show you what Religion
has to say about the solemn crisis in which you stand. Let
them persuade you to hear the Divine voice, that speaks out
of the smoke and thunder of this great convulsion.

Will you have your minister serve you in trivial matters,
and will you reject his assistance when your house is on fire?
Look at your situation, in this eventful hour that is even now
sounding over head. The unchained devil of Despotism is
loose in the land. The veil is rent from the temple of Liberty.
Over half the area of this Republic, the darkness of Barbarism has fallen at noon-day, and the Genius of America hangs
crucified among thieves! Do you want your minister to
ignore all this, lest, in the fervor of his soul, he offend somebody's scruples, and inadvertently "preach Politics?" Do
you want him to be a spaniel parasite, gliding about between
the legs of taller men, and barking for the man who will give
him the most meat? Or, do you want him to stand up as
God's freeman, testifying to what he knows, esteeming his
manhood greater than pelf, humanity more sacred than any
Church interest,—and so striving to reach the summit of the
great Occasion?

For my part, I have not waited to this hour, to make my
choice. I esteem Churches so far as they subserve the interests of right and of truth; but when they abjure these, they

forfeit the blessing of God, and the respect of man. Never fear that the free and strong assertion of righteousness will harm the Kingdom of God. If the Church is imbued with spiritual life, it will abide the shock; but, if it is marked only by a dead faith, it better be buried. No earnest man stands in the pulpit, in our time, to galvanize a corpse; and, when the event has proved that there is no life in the Church to respond to the claims of humanity—how clear it will be, that we do not belong to the body of Christ, and are not members of his!

In conclusion, I repeat what I said in this pulpit, some months ago:

Any society may secure a timid, deferential *servant* who shall repeat the truisms of morality and the pass-word of the sect, in the dull monotone of a soul caged up from heaven's liberty; but, how much better to have a self-poised, conscientious *teacher*, whose formula of ministerial duty is not borrowed, but fashioned by his own creative instinct, and who stands, not by human sufferance only, but by a divine sanction, witnessed by personal force, influence and success. A society may find "a beloved pastor," trained in all the proprieties of clerical prudence, who holds no opinions that are not marketable, and who dares not confess what ticket he votes at the presidential poll; but is it an *automaton* that people deliberately choose, to dispense for them the mysteries of the kingdom of God? When they come to the altar of prayer, burdened with the labor of life; when they fly to the tents of faith, seeking refuge from over-mastering trouble; the only soul that can speak *effectively* for them, wisely administering the sacrament of care and sorrow, must be one in habitual alliance with the spirit of God, and in the daily exercise of that liberty which invites the expression of all its convictions.

Grant that possible abuses are involved in the freedom of pulpit utterance; they are also involved in the freedom of voting. Shall we therefore abolish the ballot box? A free government invites the notorious abuse of demagoguism; but it is better to bear with the abuse than exchange it for an Austrian police; for there grows in the land, *besides* this cun-

6

brous weed, a superabounding affluence of social good, that
no military despotism is allowed to trample out. So, a free
pulpit may sometimes vex the pews ; but people know that the
man who stands in it is giving them his honest thought—the
latest child of his wedded heart and brain ; and that he con-
fides it their courteous hospitality, for the time being, whether
they are capable of loving it or not.

We suppose that no Protestant preacher assumes infallibility,
or claims to be exempt from practical errors ; but it seems to
us that the man who makes it the business of his life to study
the Gospel, and to consider the application of moral principles
to the affairs of this world, ought to be *expected* to hold clear
convictions, and to announce them with boldness and energy.
His very dogmatism may grow out of the fervor of his convictions ; and it would be wiser to trace the *processes* where
his reason has traveled, at the lofty behest of the spirit, than
rashly rebel from a *conclusion* that he may even defend with
rhetoric as rough as brickbats.   What we want, in the Christian churches, is *not* ductile ecclesiastics, polished up as Sunday
reflectors of the average decency ; but long-armed thinkers,
who can reach sardonic infidelity asleep in the pew ; and broad-
breasted evangelists, who dare fire a celestial volley into a
wicked caucus or cabinet—not fearing the stain of the powder
on their raiment, so long as the *lead* carries terror in the for-
tress of the devil.   We want in the churches, bold men, who
can face the heat of occasions, and strike when the iron is hot;
loving men, who regard their congregations too tenderly to
flatter their pride, or foster their caprices ; faithful men, who
wed their faculties and their fame to the principles of Christianity, and abide whatever fortune these may involve ; *conse-
crated* men, who—drawing their vitality from the life of God—
stand on the mountain of faith like cedars. winning vigor from
the tempest, and everlasting verdure from the sky.

ADDENDA.

[From the New York Times of May 16th.]

The Question of Slavery and the Present Rebellion.

We have insisted, from the beginning of the wicked and baseless rebellion which now agitates the country, that the question of Slavery had nothing to do with it, and that the object of this great uprising of the loyal people was—not to interfere with Slavery, but to sustain the Government and Constitution of the United States. We have been confirmed in this position, by everything said or done by the Government, in this connection. In his first Proclamation, President Lincoln declared that, in the prosecution of the measures for the suppression of the rebellion, there would be no interference with the *rights of property*. General Butler, at the very outset, returned to their masters, fugitive slaves who had fled to him for protection. We believe the general sentiment of the people commends this position of the Government.

Nevertheless, it cannot be concealed that the progress of events, always rapid in revolutions, may compel a change in the policy of the Government, as well as in the sentiment of the people, upon this subject. The Southern leaders propose to conduct this war with a most extraordinary disregard of the laws and usages of civilized warfare. They have begun, by authorizing piracy and the wholesale plunder of private property. They set prices upon the heads of loyal citizens. It can scarcely be supposed that such barbarous rules as these can be put into practical operation, without working a radical change in the spirit of the war and the sentiment of the world.

As Slavery is the most vulnerable point of the South, the time may come when the Government will be compelled, in self-defence, to inquire into its relations to that institution, in time of war. And, as pertinent to that question, we copy the following remarks on this point, made by John Quincy Adams, April 14 and 15, 1842;—they will be read with interest at the present moment:

"I believe that, so long as the Slave States are able to sustain their institutions without going abroad, or calling upon other parts of the Union to aid them, or act on the subject, so long I will consent never to interfere. I have said this, and I repeat it; but if they come to the Free States, and say to them, you must help us to keep down our slaves,—you must aid us in an insurrection and a civil war,—then I say that, *with that call comes a full and plenary power, to this House and to the Senate, over the whole subject. It is a war power.* I say it is a war power; and, when your country is actually in war, *whether it be a war of invasion or a war of insurrection, Congress has power to carry on the war, and must carry it on according to the laws of war;* and by the laws of war, an invaded country has all its laws and municipal institutions swept by the board, and martial law takes the place of them.

"This power in Congress has, perhaps, never been called into exercise under the present Constitution of the United States. But when the laws of war are in force, what, I ask, is one of these laws? It is this: that when a country is invaded, and two hostile armies are set in martial array, *the commanders of both armies have power to emancipate all the slaves in the invaded territory.* Nor is this a mere theoretic statement. The history of South America shows that the doctrine has been carried into practical execution, within the last thirty years. Slavery was abolished in Columbia, first, by the Spanish General Morillo, and, secondly, by the American General Bolivar. It was abolished by virtue of a military command given at the head of the army, and its abolition continues to be law to this day. *It was abolished by the laws of war, and not by municipal enactments;* the power was exercised by military commanders, under instructions, of course, from their respective Governments. And here I recur again to the example of General Jackson. What are you now about in Congress? You are about passing a grant to refund to General Jackson the amount of a certain fine imposed upon him by a Judge, under the laws of the State of Louisiana. You are going to refund him the money, with interest; and this you are going to do, because the imposition of the fine was unjust. And why was it unjust? Because General Jackson was acting under the laws of war, and because *the moment you place a military commander in a district which is the theatre of war, the laws of war apply to that district.*

*   *   *   *   *   *   *   *   *   *

"I might furnish a thousand proofs to show that the pretensions of gentlemen to the sanctity of their municipal institutions, under a state of actual invasion and of actual war, whether servile, civil or foreign, is wholly unfounded; and, that the laws of war do, in all such cases, take the precedence. I lay this down as the law of nations. I say that military authority takes, for the time, the place of all municipal institutions, *and Slavery among the rest;* and that, under that state of things, so far from its being true that the States where Slavery exists have the exclusive management of the subject, *not only the President of the United States, but the Commander of the Army, has power to order the universal emancipation of the slaves.* I have given here, more in detail, a principle which I have asserted on this floor before now, and of which I have no more doubt, than that you, Sir, occupy that chair. I give it in its development, in order that any gentleman, from any part of the Union, may, if he thinks proper, deny the truth of the position, and may maintain his denial; not by indignation, not by passion and fury, but by sound and sober reasoning from the laws of nations and the laws of war. And if my position can be answered and refuted, I shall receive the refutation with pleasure; I shall be glad to listen to reason, aside, as I say, from indignation and passion, And if, by the force of reasoning, my understanding can be convinced, I here pledge myself to recant what I have asserted."

*   *   *   *   *   *   *   *   *   *

There is, in this declaration, from one of the ablest publicists this country has ever known, matter worthy of profound consideration.

Its main position is, that in war the military law supersedes, and, for the moment, annuls the civil law. It is for the Commander at the head of the Army, to declare what shall be law in any military district within his control: and the only question he has to ask himself is, what will best promote the efficiency of his military operations. The moment a Federal army is marched into any Slave State, the general, at the head of it, has power to decree the emancipation of every slave.

This is a prodigious power,—one which, it is to be hoped, our armies will not be compelled to exercise. But no man can shut his eyes to the possibility,—the probability even,—that this contest will be waged, by the rebel forces, in a manner so regardless of all law, and all humanity, as to compel a resort to every weapon which the laws of war legitimately place at our command.

The South has begun, by waging *a piratical war upon private property*. In this, they take us at prodigious disadvantage. The sea is white with the sails of our commerce, and millions of dollars may be plundered, and thousands of our lives taken by their privateers, while they have no commerce exposed to retaliation. They have struck a blow at *our* "peculiar institutions,"—at commerce, in which millions upon millions of our property are invested. We suggested, some weeks ago, that the issuing of letters-of-marque would be almost certain, sooner or later, to lead to measures of retaliation upon *their* peculiar property,—the only property they have which is vulnerable to assault.

At present, public sentiment indorses, fully, the policy pursued by General Butler, and set forth in his letter to Governor Andrew. But, after the Southern privateers have fairly commenced their murderous depredations upon our commerce, it will be impossible to restrain our people from wielding every weapon which the laws of war place in their hands.

[From a Report of the Boston Anniversaries, published in the New-York *Tribune* of June 3d.]

The annual meetings, of the American Anti-Slavery Society, were postponed by the simultaneous decision of many minds, through a wise unwillingness to risk even a ripple against the grand reformatory wave which Divine Providence is now so gloriously rolling over the nation, in this magnificent war for Freedom and the Constitution.

But, glad as this people would have been to have heard the splendid orators of Anti-Slavery, whose peerless eloquence all admit and

admire, there was no need of it this year, as a specialty, when all the
speakers, at all the meetings, from the Tract Society downward, had
no other text than the War—Freedom—and Slavery. The tenor of
ever speech was War—the base was Slavery—the deep, sub-base was
Abolition.

Dr. Tyng said, before the Boston American Tract Society, that
slave-holding—that is, holding men and women in bondage—was a
crime. Hear me, added he, as they were uproarious with applause,
Slavery ought to be abolished—Slavery can be abolished—Slavery
shall be abolished—Slavery will be abolished—by this war. If to
believe that, and to work for it, is Abolitionism, then I'm an Abolitionist.

Quoting from a South-side clergyman, who argued that Slavery was
a divine institution—"Yes," said the Doctor, "as hell is a divine
institution, and destined, I hope, to go to the devil with the close of
this war."

Beyond denial, this speech of Dr. Tyng was, as *The Traveller* has
intimated, the boldest and most eloquent speech of the kind, ever
listened to by Boston orthodoxy. Middlemen and ultra conservatists,
that six months ago would have turned pale and stood aghast at such
a belching of fanaticism, now bent over and applauded to the echo
the strongest patriotic and Anti-Slavery blasts of the lion-hearted
Doctor, who seemed, as the French say, in a state of perfect *abandon*
to his theme, and yet of entire control and choice of his language.
The inspirited afflatus was plainly upon him. The sacred furore was
clear to be seen.

Abolitionists, proper, had nothing to do but leave the course clear
for such a fiery charger, whose neck was clothed with thunders by
this glorious war for the Union, the Constitution, and Freedom.
Nevertheless, at the three public meetings of the Church Anti-Slavery
Society, not a few strong things were said and done, by the Revs.
Messrs. Webster, Blanchard, Cheever, Davis, Thorne, Fee, Bailey,
Smith, Lewis Tappan, and others.

The resolutions adopted were vigorous, and wisely in advance of
those births of Providence which are rapidly ripening, and which,
there will not be wanting strength to deliver when their hour has
come. One of them declares:—

"That, in our judgment, the guiding star, through the war into which we have
been forced, is the purpose of God in regard to Slavery, as made known by His
word, His spirit, and His providence; and if our Government is still dreaming that
this struggle can be successful, while the laws of Jehovah are ignored and his command, 'LET THE OPPRESSED GO FREE,' is disregarded, then there is preparing for us
a terrible awakening."

Another resolution quotes at length from the celebrated speech of John Quincy Adams, in 1842, and asserts, with confidence, " that, in the order of Divine Providence, the time has come for the people and the Government to avail themselves of the rights of the war power, as argued by John Quincy Adams, and to *declare an act of emancipation as* the only means of averting the horrors of a wide-spread and most bloody servile insurrection."

* * * * * * * * * * * *

The Ministry and Churches were recommended to sign and circulate a memorial to the President of the United States, that, as the Chief Magistrate of the Nation—" the minister of God for good, not bearing the sword in vain,"—and having the undoubted Constitutional right, by the war power, with which he is intrusted, to "proclaim Liberty throughout all the land, unto all the inhabitants thereof,"— that he call, by proclamation, upon all the inhabitants of the United States of all conditions, bond and free, to aid in supporting the Government,—assuring them all of its impartial protection under the common flag of our National Union and Freedom.

A petition was forthwith drawn up, and signed by upward of twenty-five representative clergymen of different denominations, from all parts of the country, and forwarded to Washington.

[From a Washington letter in the New-York *Times* of May 31st.]

Probable Effect of the War upon Slavery.

The impression gains ground that there can be no end to the present war, no compromise, no peace, which leaves the cause of it in existence. The irrepressible conflict having taken this sanguinary character, can no more be staid while Slavery exists. It has been resolved, by the whole people of the North, that the Union must be preserved. The Government responds to this popular outburst of patriotism, and re-echoes it in official instructions to our Foreign Ministers. This is the one great point determined, and it is now becoming evident that it cannot be made final and sure without a complete overthrow of the institution of Slavery.

How, then, shall this great revolution in Southern society be effected? It can be accomplished by making war upon it, and nothing seems to be more probable than that abolition will be a necessary result of war. The war will cost hundreds of millions, directly and indirectly, to the Government, hundreds of millions to the rebels, and the event will leave the weaker party in a condition little short of ruin.

Is it not better to look these facts in the face, in the beginning of the contest, and make an effort at compromise, on the broad and permanent basis of peaceful and gradual emancipation, with compensation? It may be necessary that the South shall receive one or two overwhelming defeats in the battle field, before its people will consent to so radical a measure; but, in the meantime, it will be well for the people of the North to have it under consideration. If Congress should adopt a resolution in favor of calling a General Convention of the States, looking to the adoption of such a compromise, it could not fail at once to arrest the attention of thousands of Southern men, who would prefer such a settlement to a continuance of destructive war.

If, for instance, it were agreed that Slavery should be abolished at the end of ten years, and, in the meantime, to be greatly modified and improved in its grosser features, on condition that the owners should receive, in United States' Stocks, an average of one hundred dollars per head for their slaves, the alternative would be seized with joy, by a large portion of the Southern people. The cost of this arrangement, to the Government, would be about four hundred millions of dollars, which is less than a war of four years would cost to either party.

Provision for the abolition of Slavery at the end of ten years, would give no shock, immediate or remote, to the frame-work of society, even in a time of profound peace and prosperity; and in the actual circumstances of the case with a destructive war raging, which abolition would put an end to, it would be the very best thing the South could do, even without compensation. The sum, proposed to be paid to the slave-holders, is probably not more than one-fourth of the cash value of the slaves before the rebellion commenced; but it is fully half their value at the present moment, and is more than they would fetch a year hence, if the war continues. It is also to be an advance payment, for the liberation of the slaves at the end of ten years. With that ready capital, the South would at once enter upon a career of prosperity and progress unparalleled in its previous history, and the North would be more than compensated for its share in the burden, by the revival of business.

www.ingramcontent.com/pod-product-compliance
Lightning Source LLC
Chambersburg PA
CBHW021428090426
42739CB00009B/1392